Red, Blue, and Yellow, too!

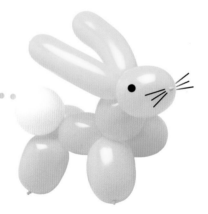

SCHOLASTIC

Children's Press®
A Division of Scholastic Inc.
New York Toronto London Auckland Sydney
Mexico City New Delhi Hong Kong
Danbury, Connecticut

**Early Childhood
Consultants:**

Ellen Booth Church
Diane Ohanesian

1 2 3 4 5 6 7 8 9 10 R 19 18 17 16 15 14 13 12 11 10   62

Library of Congress Cataloging-in-Publication Data

  Red, blue, and yellow, too!
    p. cm. — (Rookie preschool)
  ISBN-13: 978-0-531-24403-6 (lib. bdg.)   ISBN-13: 978-0-531-24578-1 (pbk.)
  ISBN-10: 0-531-24403-2 (lib. bdg.)   ISBN-10: 0-531-24578-0 (pbk.)
  1. Colors—Juvenile literature. I. Title. II. Series
   QC495.5.R433 2010
   535.6 – dc22   2009005794

The clouds roll in.
The sky turns gray.

Drip, drip, drip.
It's a rainy day.

Out in the rain
and getting wet,

this **PURPLE** pig
is not upset.

Two BLUE puppies jump and run.

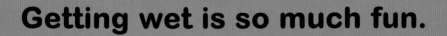

Getting wet is so much fun.

These GREEN turtles
love the rain.

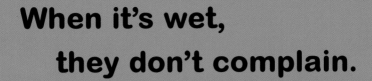

When it's wet, they don't complain.

YELLOW rabbits
splash and hop,

waiting for the rain to stop.

Raindrops splatter on the ground.

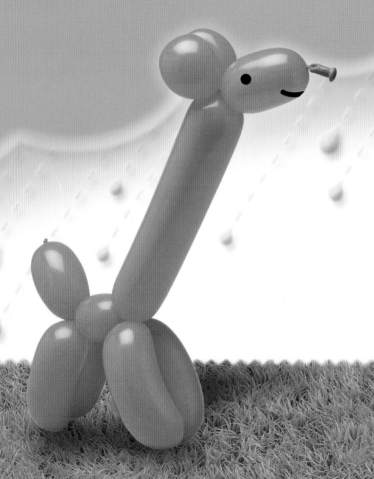

ORANGE giraffes
hear the sound.

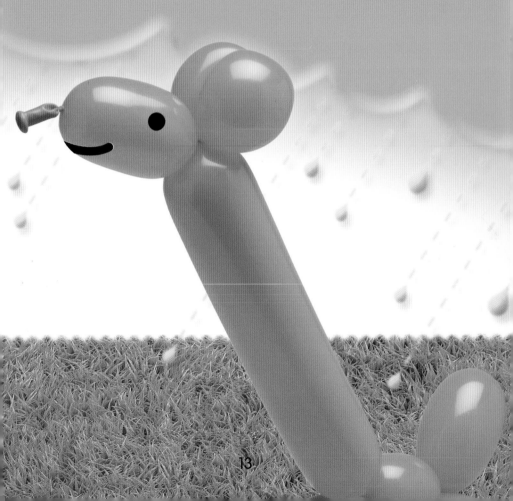

A big RED elephant comes stomping through,

making noise
and spraying, too.

The rain is stopping.
It's getting dry.

The sun starts lighting up the sky.

All the animals run and play.

Hooray!

It's a perfect

rainbow day!

Rookie Storytime Tips

. . . .

Red, Blue, and Yellow, Too! presents color and weather concepts in a playful way. As you and your child enjoy the book together, ask him or her to name the colors of the animals on each page. Talk about the unusual colors of the clouds. This is a great way to start a lively conversation about colors in the world!

. . . .

Invite your child to go back through the book and look for what follows. Along the way, he or she will build visual discrimination and color recognition skills.

What colors do you
see in the rainbow?

Can you match each animal to its color
in the rainbow?

Look out the window. Do you see clouds? What color are they? Do the shapes remind you of any animals?